COOKING UP FUN

with Jodie Fitz

Illustrations by Rich Conley

The illustrations in this book were made with
creativity, imagination, ink, digital technology and LOVE.

ISBN-10: 0-990337324
ISBN-13: 978-0-9903373-2-4

Published in 2015 by
Saratoga Springs Publishing, L.L.C.
Saratoga Springs, NY
SaratogaSpringsPublishing@gmail.com
www.SaratogaSpringsPublishing.com

Written and Created by Jodie Fitz
www.jodiefitz.com
www.facebook.com/jodiefitzcooks
www.instagram.com/jodiefitz
www.twitter.com/jodiefitz
www.pinterest.com/jodiefitzcooks

Saratoga Springs Publishing's books are available at special discounts when purchased
in quantity for premiums and promotions as well as fundraising or educational use.

Special editions can also be created to specification.

For details or to purchase any of our products
please contact us at:
www.SaratogaSpringsPublishing.com

Front cover photograph by Matt Hunziker.
Back cover photograph by Teri Sholtz.

Dedicated to my three children who I have enjoyed sharing crazy recipes with throughout the years. Not only do I love watching you grow into wonderful individuals, you have inspired much of my creativity. And, to my loving husband who always puts up with my kitchen experiments whether they are a 'thumbs up or thumbs down' in the end. You all make my life complete, both in & out of the kitchen. As they say... 'I love you ALL to the moon & back!'

As always, there are a lot of people to celebrate in my life & I wish I could mention each and every one of you. But, I want to make a special shout out to Rich Conley, my friend & artist extraordinaire who brought this book to life with amazing pictures throughout. And, to Brad Nutting who not only helped with the layout of this book, but who my kids enjoy having at the counters & who I appreciate being part of many taste testing moments. We will all miss you when your college time has ended, but will always wish you the best that life has to offer.

To Vicki... you are truly talented, amazing at all that you do & I appreciate this opportunity to work with you; not only on this project but with all that we have planned. I am thankful to have had the privilege to get to know you & am thankful for your friendship and encouragment.

HEY KIDS! This cookbook is meant to be interactive. Not only do you get to make the recipes & have your own taste tesing fun; you also get to color each page & vote on each recipe by circling a 'thumbs up' or 'thumbs down'. Send me a note and/or a picture of the recipes you make from the book at jodie@jodiefitz.com ~ I would love to hear about your kitchen adventures.

TABLE OF CONTENTS

Smoothies & Fun Drinks

Breakfast YUM

Snackin' Ideas

Lunch & Dinner are Served

SMOOTHIES & FUN DRINKS...

APPLE BANANA SMOOTHIE

1 1/2 cups low-fat milk
1 apple
1 banana, frozen*
1 cup ice
1/4 cup peanut butter
1 tablespoon honey
1 teaspoon vanilla extract
1/2 teaspoon cinnamon

Wash and peel the apple. Core the apple. Cut the apples into slices and place it into the blender. Add the banana, ice, low-fat milk, peanut butter, honey, vanilla extract and cinnamon. Blend and serve. This recipe is a great for a quick and easy breakfast or afterschool snack.

*Frozen Bananas: Peel the banana and slice it. Place the banana slices on a waxed paper covered plate and cover them with another piece of waxed paper on top and freeze them the night before. If you don't freeze the bananas ahead of time, simply add three cups of ice instead of one.

* Honey: You may need to adjust the amount of honey needed in this recipe depending on the type and brand of peanut butter used.

2

 Did you like this recipe?

BERRY BLASTER SMOOTHIE

3 cups frozen Berry Medley
1 1/2 cups low-fat milk
6 oz. vanilla yogurt, low-fat
1 1/2 – 2 tablespoons honey
1 teaspoon raspberry extract
1 teaspoon lime juice
1/2 teaspoon vanilla extract

Add the frozen berries, milk, vanilla yogurt, honey, raspberry extract, vanilla extract and lime juice to the blender. Mix well & serve. This recipe is great for a breakfast on the run or a quick & easy snack.

*Frozen Berry Medley contains fresh frozen strawberries, blueberries, raspberries and blackberries with no added syrups or sugars.

 Did you like this recipe?

CASTLE MOAT

2 cups ice
1 cup low-fat milk
1 tablespoon cocoa powder
1 teaspoon vanilla extract
1/4 cup honey

Add the ice, milk, cocoa powder,
vanilla extract & honey into a
blender. Blend the ingredients until
the ice is fully crushed & the
ingredients are well mixed.

Note: You may have to stop half way through the blending process and scrape
cocoa powder & honey from the sides with a spatula and then continue to blend
the rest of the way.

4

 Did you like this recipe?

CHOCO MONKEY SMOOTHIE

1 banana
1 cup low-fat milk
2 cups ice
1 tablespoon cocoa powder
1 1/2 teaspoons vanilla extract
1 teaspoon cinnamon
2 tablespoons honey
2 - 4 tablespoons creamy peanut butter

Peel and slice the banana, add the banana, milk, ice, cocoa powder, vanilla extract, cinnamon, honey and peanut butter into the blender and mix thoroughly.

DID YOU KNOW?!?

There is a monkey called a spider monkey? The Spider Monkey is an omnivore, but mostly eats fruits and nuts.

 Did you like this recipe?

FROZEN LEMONADE YUM

4 cups ice
2 lemons, fresh
2 cups water
2 teaspoons raspberry extract
1 teaspoon vanilla extract
1/2 cup honey

Cut the lemons in half to create four halves. Squeeze the lemon juice from the lemons. If you have a citrus squeezer simply squeeze it right into a blender pitcher. If you do the lemon squeezing by hand, simply squeeze the juice into a liquid measuring cup so that you can extract the seeds from the juice before pouring the juice into the blender.

Add the ice, water, extracts and honey together with the fresh lemon juice in a blender & blend. It's delicious and fresh to serve.

Optional: Add 5 – 7 fresh frozen blueberries into the frozen lemonade & the lemonade will turn a beautiful color, which is fun any time

Did you like this recipe?

IGUANA SLUSH

3/4 cup fresh squeezed lime juice
1 cup water
4 cups ice
1/2 cup honey
2 teaspoons vanilla extract

Add the fresh squeezed lime juice, water, ice, honey and vanilla extract to a blender and blend. Mix until the consistency is that of a lime slush drink.

* You will get more juice from the limes using a citrus squeezer. However, you can hand press it. And, by squeezing the lime in different directions, extract the same amount of juice.

Did you like this recipe?

LAVA JUICE

6 oz. pineapple juice
1/4 cup POM cherry juice
1/2 teaspoon vanilla extract
2 tablespoons honey
1 cup ice
Cherry Seltzer

Add the ice, pineapple juice, cherry juice, vanilla extract and honey in to a blender and blend. Pour a 1/2 cup of seltzer into four, 10 oz. glasses. Pour the Lava Juice mixture on top of the seltzer and serve.

Optional: Top it off with a maraschino cherry. Or, even better... a fresh pitted cherry!

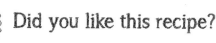 Did you like this recipe?

RAINBOW SMOOTHIE

Red = 2 cups strawberries, fresh frozen
Purple = 6 oz. blackberry yogurt, low-fat
Blue = 1 cup blueberries, fresh frozen
Green = 1 cup spinach, fresh baby leaf
Yellow = 1 tablespoon of fresh squeezed lemon juice
Orange = 1/2 navel orange
Pot of Gold = 2 tablespoons honey
Dash of Magic = 1 teaspoon vanilla extract
2 1/2 cups low-fat milk

Add the strawberries, yogurt, blueberries and spinach into the blender. Cut a lemon in half, remove the seeds and squeeze one tablespoon of fresh lemon juice to add to the smoothie. Simply squeeze the rind together of the naval orange to add as much fresh orange juice to the smoothie as possible; twist as you squeeze & try squeezing from the opposite direction to press the juice out. Add in the honey, vanilla and milk. Blend & serve. This recipe makes a delicious and thick smoothie to share.

DID YOU KNOW?!?

...that a rainbow appears when light is bent in water droplets in the atmosphere? A rainbow is not an object, it cannot be approached or physically touched.

 Did you like this recipe?

STRAWBERRIED MILK

1 cup frozen fresh strawberries (no syrup added)
1 cup low-fat or fat free milk
1 teaspoon vanilla extract
3 tablespoons honey

Add the strawberries, milk, vanilla extract and honey into a blender. Blend the ingredients until the strawberries are fully crushed and mixed thoroughly into the recipe.

 Note: Occasionally you may have to stop the blending process mid-way through to scrape the honey from the sides and then continue the process.

DID YOU KNOW?!?
...that Strawberries are the only fruit that wear their seeds on the outside. And, Strawberries are members of the rose family.

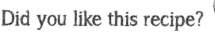

Did you like this recipe?

TROPICAL BEACH SMOOTHIE

1 cup vanilla coconut milk
6 oz. pineapple juice
6 oz. vanilla yogurt, low-fat
3 cups ice
1/2 banana
1 mango
1 tablespoon honey
1 teaspoon vanilla extract

Peel and slice the banana. Cut the mango and remove the skin. Add the coconut milk, pineapple juice, yogurt, ice, banana, mango, honey and vanilla extract into a blender and mix thoroughly.

HOW TO CUT A MANGO: The mango has a large seed in the center. Using a sharp knife, an adult can slice the sides off on either side of the nut, which is typically the widest side starting at the top of the stem. If the mango is ripe, children can use a plastic knife to cut squares into the cut sides. I like to tell them it's like drawing a 'tic tac toe' board with more lines; a grid. Then, they can scoop out the cubes of mango with a spoon.

IS MY MANGO RIPE? Making this smoothie provides a great opportunity in teaching children about how to tell when a mango is ripe or not. Is it soft or hard? If you can press on the fruit and feel its softness, it is ripe and ready to make the Tropical Smoothie. If it's hard, it's not ready and needs to sit for another day or two.

HALF BANANA: What do you do with the other half of the banana? Eat it! Or, cover it with waxed paper and save it for another Smoothie.

Did you like this recipe?

BREAKFAST YUM!

BAGEL FLOWERS

1 mini bagel, whole grain
2 tablespoons mascarpone cheese
1/4 teaspoon vanilla extract
1 teaspoon honey
Fresh strawberries
Fresh pineapple

Stir the mascarpone cheese, vanilla extract and honey together. Rinse and slice the strawberries. Open the bagel and spread the mascarpone cheese on the inside of both halves of the bagel. Lay the strawberries on one side to create strawberry flowers pedals. Close the bagel and put the pineapple piece into the center of the bagel.

DID YOU KNOW?!?

Did You Know that the Wolffia flower is the smallest flower in the world? it also produces the world's smallest fruit, called a utricle. And, the worlds largest flower can grow to be 3 feet across and weigh up to 15 pounds!

 Did you like this recipe?

BREAKFAST BURRITOS

Turkey breakfast sausage links, cooked
Turkey bacon, cooked
Ham, cooked
8 eggs, large
6 – tortilla wraps
8 oz. sharp cheddar, shredded

1 tablespoon canola oil
1/4 teaspoon onion powder
1/8 teaspoon black pepper
Mild Salsa
Non-stick cooking spray

Scramble the eggs together in a bowl with the onion powder & black pepper. Cook them in scrambled fashion using the non-stick cooking spray.

After you have cooked the sausage, cooked the bacon & browned the cooked ham, simply cut them into small-diced pieces.

Fill the center of each burrito with eggs, meat, salsa & approximately 2 tablespoons of cheese. Roll them as you would a burrito.

If you are going to cook them right away, place them seam down, in a glass-baking dish that has been coated with the non-stick cooking spray. Baste the top of each burrito with the canola oil & top them with shredded cheese. Cook them in a pre-heated oven at 375 degrees for approximately 10 minutes; until they are golden brown on the edges. Serve warm with a side of fresh fruit.

If you are going to freeze the burritos, place each burrito you have just rolled on a baking sheet that is lined with parchment paper. Place the tray of burritos into the freezer and let them freeze for at least one hour. Remove the tray, wrap each one individually with parchment paper and place them in an airtight freezing container or a freezer storage bag. When you are ready for your burritos, simply remove them for the freezer and let them set while you are heating the oven. Follow the direction above to baste, top with cheese & bake before serving.

  Did you like this recipe?

BREAKFAST DELIGHTS

4 eggs
1/4 cup low-fat milk
3 tablespoons honey
1 1/2 teaspoon cinnamon
1 teaspoon vanilla extract
6 – 9 slices of bread*
Butter or non-stick cooking spray

Whip together the eggs, milk, honey cinnamon & vanilla extract. Prepare the bread by stacking three slices at a time, remove the crust and cut them into long strips. I typically am able to cut three strips per slice.

Then simply soak the slices in the egg mixture turning them so that all sides are fully coated. Cook them on a coated griddle with either butter or a non-stick cooking spray like you would a traditional slice of French Toast, until it is fully cooked through & toasted on all sides; use medium to low heat.

*Use your favorite whole wheat bread; sometimes we use the honey wheat bread. The amount of slices of bread that can be used in this recipe will depend on how long you let them soak in the egg mixture.

What's on Top? These are delicious enough to eat alone! However, you can also try dunking them in a low-fat vanilla yogurt or thawing fresh frozen fruit with no sugars added to put on top. When the fruit thaws it creates its own juice that's naturally sweet and perfect for serving with this type of recipe.

 Did you like this recipe?

FRUITY PARFAIT YUM

6 oz. low-fat vanilla yogurt
1/2 cup frozen Berry Medley, thawed
2 tablespoons Grape Nut cereal or granola

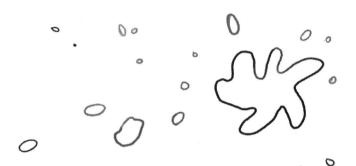

Place 3 oz. of the yougurt into a parfait glass. Add 1/4 cup of the berries and one tablespoon of the cereal. Add the remaing 3 oz. of yogurt into the parfait glass. Finish off the parfait with a final layer of the remaining 1/4 cup of berries and one more tablespoon of cereal.

Did you like this recipe?

HIDDEN GEMS

1 tablespoon tapioca
2 cups mixed berries, frozen
1 teaspoon cinnamon
2 whole grain tortilla wraps
2 tablespoons fat free cream cheese, softened
1 tablespoon honey
Non-stick cooking spray

Yogurt Glaze:

3 oz. low-fat vanilla yogurt
1 tablespoon fat free milk
1 tablespoon honey

Pre-heat oven to 375 degrees.

Stir the frozen berries, tapioca and cinnamon together. Set aside. Mix the cream cheese and one tablespoon of honey together. Spread a thin layer of the cream cheese and honey mixture onto each tortilla. Pour half of the berry mixture onto half of one tortilla and then repeat on the other tortilla. Fold the tortillas like a taco and place them onto a non-stick baking sheet sprayed with the non-stick cooking spray. Bake for 15 minutes.

Stir the yogurt, 1 tablespoon of honey and milk together. Top each taco with a drizzle of the yogurt sauce and serve warm.

 Did you like this recipe?

HOMERUN QUESADILLA

2 - 8" flour tortillas
2 eggs, large
3 tablespoons milk, low-fat
1/2 cup pepper jack cheese, shredded
2 tablespoons salsa (optional)
salt & pepper to taste
non-stick cooking spray
butter, room temperature

Crack the eggs into a glass bowl that has been coated with non-stick cooking spray.

Season the eggs with salt & pepper to taste.
Add the milk to the eggs and whisk the eggs, salt, pepper & milk together.
Place the glass bowl into the microwave and cook it on high for one minute.
Carefully remove the glass dish & stir the eggs together to scramble them. If they are not fully cooked, return the glass dish to the microwave for 30 seconds and stir again; repeat if needed.

If desired, stir two tablespoons of salsa into the eggs.
Spread a thin layer of butter onto one side of one of the tortillas and place it butter side down onto a griddle style pan. Evenly add a layer of eggs and then top it off with the shredded cheese.

Place the remaining wrap on top & lightly butter the top layer.
Cook the quesadilla over medium heat as if you were cooking a grilled cheese; until both sides are lightly browned & the cheese is fully melted.
You can cut the breakfast quesadilla into wedges with a pizza cutter and serve with a side dish of fruit or serve it as a Home Run Hit by using either Siracha Sauce or Taco Sauce to create baseball lines on one side of an uncut breakfast quesadilla. The Siracha Sauce can typically be purchased in a squeeze bottle ready to create lines easily. The taco sauce will need to be transferred into a cake-decorating utensil with a large writing tip in order to create the lines.

 Did you like this recipe?

HOT DIGGITY DOG BREAKFAST

6 turkey breakfast sausage, fully cooked
4 eggs
1/4 cup low-fat milk
1/2 teaspoon onion powder
1/4 teaspoon salt
1/4 teaspoon pepper
Non-stick cooking spray

Slice the cooked turkey sausage.

Crack the eggs into a bowl. Add the milk, onion powder, salt & pepper.
Whisk it all together.

Coat a griddle style pan with non-stick cooking spray. Add the cut sausages
to the pan & heat the pan over medium to low heat. Add the eggs over the
sausage & move the eggs around as they cook with a spatula to make
scrambled eggs with sausage.

Serve with your favorite whole wheat toast, mini bagel or English muffin and
fruit.

 Did you like this recipe?

MARTIAN MUNCHIES

1 package of pre-made mini fillo shells
3 eggs
1/8 cup low-fat milk
3 - 6 oz. sharp cheddar cheese, shredded
1/2 cups spinach, fresh baby leaves
1/4 teaspoon salt
1/4 teaspoon pepper
1/8 teaspoon onion powder

Crack the eggs into a blender. Add in the milk, spinach, pepper, salt, onion powder and blend until the eggs have turned green and there are not any visible spinach leaves.

Place the mini fillo shells on to a baking sheet or in a mini muffin pan. Fill each fillo shell 3/4 full with the egg mixture . Bake for 20-30 minutes; until the eggs are fully cooked. Top each one with cheese and continue to cook for 5 minutes longer; until the cheese is melted. Serve warm.

 Did you like this recipe?

RAINFOREST BREAD

1/2 cup sugar
1/2 cup applesauce
1/4 cup butter, softened
2 large eggs
1 teaspoon vanilla extract
1-1/2 cups zucchini, shredded
1/4 cup carrots, shredded
1/4 cup orange juice
2 cups flour
1/2 teaspoon baking soda
1/4 teaspoon salt
1/2 teaspoon cinnamon
1/2 teaspoon baking powder
3/4 cups raisins

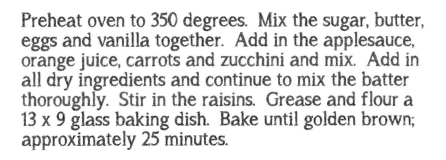

Preheat oven to 350 degrees. Mix the sugar, butter, eggs and vanilla together. Add in the applesauce, orange juice, carrots and zucchini and mix. Add in all dry ingredients and continue to mix the batter thoroughly. Stir in the raisins. Grease and flour a 13 x 9 glass baking dish. Bake until golden brown; approximately 25 minutes.

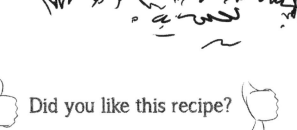

Did you like this recipe?

21

VOLCANIC PANCAKES

1 egg
1 1/2 cups flour
1 1/2 - 2 cups milk
1 tablespoon baking powder
1 teaspoon vanilla extract
1/2 teaspoon salt
1/2 cup dark chocolate mini morsels
Fresh Frozen Strawberries, thawed
Greek Vanilla yogurt

Beat the egg until it's fluffy. Combine the flour, milk, chocolate syrup, vanilla, baking powder and salt. Mix until smooth. Using a spoon, stir in the chocolate morsels. Cook the pancakes in typical four inch circle fashion.

Once they are cooked, beginning at one edge, cut into the center of the pancake with a knife and then cut out a hole at the center; you can use a knife or punch a whole using an apple corer. This is so that you can wrap & stand the pancake like a cone on a plate.

Place the Greek yogurt in a ziploc bag, clip the corner of one end & pipe some of it into the center & over the top. Place the strawberries in a mini chopper or food processor & puree the strawberries. Drizzle the strawberries over the top of the volcanic pancake before serving.

The Milk: if you use 1 1/2 cups of milk, the pancakes will be thick & fluffy. If you add the additional 1/2 cup of milk, they will be thinner.

Did you like this recipe?

SNACKIN' IDEAS...

CAT TAILS

2 bananas
1 cup chocolate morsels
2 tablespoons peanut butter
2 tablespoons grape nut cereal
4 wooden craft sticks

Peel and cut the bananas in half. Insert a wooden craft stick into the bottom so that only two inches of the stick is exposed. Place the bananas on to a waxed paper lined plate and place them in the freezer for approximately an hour.

Put the chocolate and peanut butter into a glass bowl and microwave for one minute. Stir the chocolate and peanut butter together. Add in the cereal and stir. Dip the bananas into the chocolate mixture. Return the bananas to the waxed paper lined plate and put them into the freezer for ten minutes and serve.

WHAT TO DO IF YOU HAVE AN EXTRA CAT TAIL?:
If you wrap it in waxed paper and place it in a freezer storage bag, it can be saved for another day.

Did you like this recipe?

CATERPILLAR CRUNCH

1 banana
¾ cup GrapeNut Cereal
1/3 cup peanut butter
1 tablespoon honey
1 tablespoon wheat germ
½ teaspoon cinnamon
1/8 teaspoon vanilla extract
Small Pretzel Sticks
Raisins

Place the peanut butter in a glass bowl and microwave it for at 30 seconds on high. Stir the honey, wheat germ, cinnamon and vanilla extract into the peanut butter. Peel and slice the banana. Fold the banana pieces into the peanut butter mixture so that they are fully covered with the peanut butter mixture, but still banana rounds. Roll the peanut butter covered banana slices in the Grape Nut cereal so that they are fully coated. Place the banana rounds on a plate and let them set in the refrigerator.

Create a caterpillar by connecting three rounds together with small pretzels sticks as the connectors to create the body. Place one round on top of the first round with a small pretzel stick connecting them to serve as the caterpillar head. Add two raisins as eyes by spreading peanut butter on one side and sticking them into place. Break a small pretzel stick in half and add them into the head as antennae.

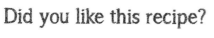

Did you like this recipe?

FIRE FLY FOOD

6 oz. slivered almonds
5 oz. blueberry Craisins
1/2 cup pitted dates
1/2 cup old-fashioned rolled oats
1/4 cup sunflower seeds, salted
3 tablespoons flaxseed
3 tablespoons honey
1/2 teaspoon vanilla extract
Non-stick cooking spray

Coat an 8×8 glass dish with a heavy coat of non-stick cooking spray.

Add the almonds, blueberry Craisins, pitted dates, rolled oats, sunflower seeds, flaxseed, honey and vanilla extract into a food processor. Mix the ingredients together thoroughly by using the pulsating feature.

Pour the mixture into the pre-coated glass dish. Using a spoon, press the mixture tightly into the dish evenly and tightly. Place the glass dish into the refrigerator and let set for one hour. Cut the recipe into equal sized bars. Using a spatula, remove each bar from the pan and place them in an airtight storage container with waxed paper in between layers for storing.

 Did you like this recipe?

FRUITALICIOUS YUM

2 tablespoons Vanilla yogurt, low-fat
1 tablespoon Greek Vanilla yogurt, non-fat
4 cherries, fresh frozen/thawed
1 teaspoon walnuts, chopped (optional)
1 medium banana

Chop the cherries either in a mini chopper or with a knife. Stir the yogurts, cherries and nuts (if desired) together. Send it to school in a small container with a banana. You can simply peel the banana, dip & eat. Or, for after school, slice the banana and use pretzel sticks as edible skewers to serve.

Serving it to Guests: If you want to serve this recipe to guests simply modify the dip as follows; 1/2 cup low-fat vanilla yogurt, 1/4 cup non-fat Greek vanilla yogurt, 16 fresh frozen cherries thawed and 1/8 cup chopped walnuts. Combine the ingredients as directed above.

Frozen Cherries: We used thawed frozen cherries because they are pitted and when they thaw they naturally release juice to color the yogurts and add a delicious flavor.

 Did you like this recipe?

GOBBLE UPS

4 cups multi-grain Cheerio's
1 cup crunchy peanut butter
3 tablespoons honey

2 teaspoons cocoa powder
1 teaspoon vanilla

Melt the peanut butter in a glass dish in the microwave on high for one minute. Add the honey, cocoa powder and vanilla extract to the peanut butter and stir the ingredients together until they are mixed together thoroughly. Add the peanut butter mixture to the cereal and stir until the cereal is coated with the peanut butter mixture.

Line a baking sheet with waxed paper. Roll the cereal mixture into ball shapes and place them on the baking sheet. Let the cereal crunch set in the refrigerator for at least one hour.

Peanut Butter: We use a natural/organic peanut butter. However, you can make adjustments in the honey to add or decrease the sweetness depending on your favorite peanut butter.

Make Ahead: This is a great recipe to make the night before and have ready to cut and serve as part of a breakfast. It's great served with fruit and a glass of milk or with a side of yogurt.

Cereal: This recipe can also be made with Honey Nut Cheerio, Cinnamon Cheerio cereals or other similar cereal alternatives.

GOBBLE GOBBLE GOBBLE Gobble Gobble Gobble Gobble GOBBLE GOBBLE GOBBLE GOBBLE

Did you like this recipe?

GRASSHOPPER FREEZE

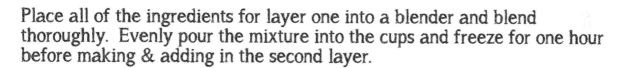

You will need three 5 oz. paper cups and three craft sticks to make this recipe.

Layer One:
6 oz. low-fat vanilla yogurt
1/8 cup green spinach leaves
1 tablespoon honey
1 - 2 drops mint extract
1/2 teaspoon vanilla extract

Place all of the ingredients for layer one into a blender and blend thoroughly. Evenly pour the mixture into the cups and freeze for one hour before making & adding in the second layer.

Layer Two:
6 oz. low-fat vanilla yogurt
2 tablespoons honey
1 tablespoon cocoa powder
1/2 teaspoon vanilla extract

Fold the yogurt, honey, cocoa powder and vanilla extract together. Let the yogurt set for at least 15 minutes. Add the second layer to the pops, insert the craft sticks and let the pops set overnight before removing the cup and serving.

You can either cut the cup off or run it under warm water to release the pop from the paper cup.

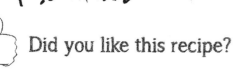

 Did you like this recipe?

MAGIC APPLES

1 apple
2 tablespoons peanut butter
    (creamy or crunchy will work)
1 tablespoon honey (optional)
1/2 teaspoon cinnamon
1/4 teaspoon cocoa powder

Pre-heat the oven to 375 degrees.
Using an apple slicer/corer, cut the apple 80% to the bottom. Remove the apple slicer/corer and carefully cut or spoon the core from the center of the apple. The goal is to keep the bottom of the apple intact so that you have a hollowed center that you can fill.

Stir the peanut butter, honey, cinnamon & cocoa powder together. Fill the center of the apple with the peanut butter mixture. Wrap the apple in foil and bake for 20 minutes.

Let the apple cool just enough to peel the wedges covered in peanut butter and eat them or scoop out the apple and eat it with a spoon while it's hot.

 Did you like this recipe?

MINI FLOWER POTS

3 oz. low-fat strawberry yogurt
3 oz. low-fat blueberry yogurt
3 oz. Greek vanilla yogurt, non-fat
1 package frozen mini fillo cups
Strawberries
Blueberries

Thaw the fillo cups.

Rinse the strawberries, remove the greens and slice them; set aside.

Rinse the blueberries and set aside.

In a bowl, fold the yogurts together.
Fill each fillo cup with some of the yogurt mixture.

Lay 3 – 5 slices of strawberries around the top, dipping the larger end of the strawberry into the yogurt with the pointier end sticking out as if they are pedals on a flower. Add a blueberry to the center of each flower.

 Did you like this recipe?

PINWHEELS

1 English Muffin, honey wheat
1 medium Apple
4 oz. Monterey Jack Cheese, shredded
1 teaspoon cinnamon
Honey
Non-stick cooking spray

Preheat the oven to 400 degrees.
Cut the English muffin in half separating the top from the bottom so that you have two circles. In a separate bowl mix the cheese and cinnamon together; set aside. Wash, core and thinly slice the apple leaving the skin.

Lay the English muffin halves onto a non stick baking sheet that hs been coated with non-stick cooking spray. Drizzle a very small amount of honey onto each muffin half. Sprinkle the cheese and cinnamon mixture over the honey and then add the apple slices in a pin wheel design. Bake in the oven for 5-7 minutes, until the cheese is melted and the English Muffin halves are crunchy.

DID YOU KNOW?!?

...that the pinwheel was created by a woman in California? The first name for a Pinwheel toy was called a Whirligig.

Did you like this recipe?

SWEET SNACKING SCEPTERS

4 oz. Greek vanilla yogurt, non-fat
6 oz. raspberry yogurt
1/4 teaspoon raspberry extract
Watermelon
Raspberries or blackberries, fresh
Blueberries, fresh
Mini heart cookie or fondant cutter (approximately 2 inches in width)
Wooden Skewers

Fold together the Greek yogurt, the raspberry yogurt and raspberry extract to create the dip. Cover and refrigerate the dip until its time to serve.

Measure the slices of watermelon to match the width of the cookie/fondant cutter you are using. The slices should be slightly less in width than the utensil you are using, but still wide enough to skew without them breaking.

Simply cut hearts out of the watermelon slices. You should be able to yield 3 hearts per slice of watermelon when using a quartered watermelon; although it will depend on the wedge sizes.

Wash the blueberries and raspberries.

Create Sweet Snackin' Sceptors by skewing three watermelon hearts with either a blueberry or raspberry/blackberry in between each one.

Serve with the dip.

 Did you like this recipe?

CAPTAIN'S CRUNCH CHICKEN

1 cup honey roasted peanuts
1 tablespoon paprika
1 1/2 teaspoons onion powder
1 teaspoon garlic powder
3/4 teaspoon salt
1/2 black pepper
1/4 teaspoon cayenne pepper
2 eggs
1/8 cup low fat milk
1 1/2 lbs. chicken strips
3 tablespoons canola or light olive oil

Serve with a Simple & Quick Honey Mustard Spread:

3 tablespoons of mayonnaise (we use the Cain's all natural)
1 tablespoon low-fat milk
1 tablespoon Gulden's mustard
1 tablespoon honey

Simply fold the ingredients together before using as a spread.

Preheat the oven to 400 degrees.

Coat the bottom of a 13 x 9 glass-baking dish with the 3 tablespoons of canola or light olive oil.

Whisk the eggs and milk together in one dish.

Finely chop the honey-roasted peanuts in a mini chopper; breadcrumb like consistency. Stir the finely chopped nuts, paprika, onion powder, garlic powder, slat, pepper & cayenne pepper together.

Coat each chicken strip first in the egg & milk mixture; this is called dredging. Then dip each piece into the nut/spice mixture.
Once they are fully coated, lay them in the glass-baking dish. Bake for approximately 25 minutes; until fully cooked.

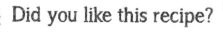 Did you like this recipe?

FLYING SAUCERS

2 slices honey wheat bread
1/2 banana
1-1/2 to 2 tablespoons peanut butter
1 teasoon honey
1 teaspoon honey
1 teaspoon vanilla extract

Stir the peanut butter, honey and extract together. Set the mixture aside.

Using a round cookie cutter, small bowl or cup that is four inches in diameter, push the round circle into the bread to create a stencil. Cut the bread with clean pair of kitchen scissors or a sharp knife so that you have two round slices of bread. Spread the peanut butter mixture on to one slice of the bread.

Slice the banana and place the sliced banana on the peanut butter leaving room around the edges. Place the second slice on top to create a sandwich. Seal the two slices of bread together by using a fork to go around and press the edges together tightly.

DID YOU KNOW?!?

...that a flying saucer is also know as an UFO; unidentified flying object? This phrase was coined in 1947.

Jupiter

Did you like this recipe?

LAVA ASHED POTATOES

4 long white potatoes
1/2 cup light olive oil
1 teaspoon sea salt
1 tablespoon paprika

Pre-heat the oven to 400 degrees.
Peel and rinse the potatoes. Slice the potatoes so that they are thin (less than 1/8 of an inch). Set aside.

In a bowl, stir together the oil, paprika and salt. Stir in the potatoes and mix until the mixture is evenly distributed.

Coat a baking pan with a very thin layer of olive oil using a paper towel. Set the slices of potatoes on the pan in a single layer. Add an additional light layer of paprika and sea salt to the top of the potatoes. Bake until golden brown, approximately 20 – 25 minutes.

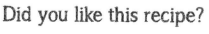 Did you like this recipe?

MOON ROCK SOUP

1 pound ground turkey
1 cup parmesan cheese, finely grated
1/2 cup + 2 tablespoons sweet onion,
finely chopped
8 oz. pasta rings
8 oz. star shapped pastina
32 oz. chicken broth
32 oz. water
1 1/2 cups finely cut carrots
3 cups baby leaf spinach
4 eggs
1 1/2 teaspoons salt
3/4 teaspoons onion powder
1/2 teaspoon garlic powder
1/2 teaspoon ground thyme
1/2 teaspoon pepper

Make mini meatballs by combining the ground turkey, finely grated parmesan cheese and 1/2 cup of onion together. Mix the ingredients thoroughly and shape them into meatballs no larger than one inch.

Pour the chicken broth and water into a large pan.
As you make the moon rock meatballs add them to the chicken broth.
After you have added all of the moon rock meatballs, bring the broth to a boil and let them simmer on high in the broth for 30 minutes.

Pre-cook the pasta as directed on the package, drain the water and set aside. Chop the spinach in a mini food processor so that it is finely chopped. Add the spinach, carrots, two tablespoons of onion, salt, onion powder, garlic powder, ground thyme and pepper to the soup, stir and simmer until the carrots and onions are tender.

Scramble the eggs in a separate bowl and add to the soup; stir as they cook. Cook for 10 minutes.

Add the pasta to your colorful galaxy mix, season to taste with additional salt and pepper if desired and serve.

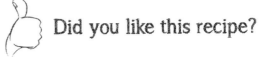 Did you like this recipe?

PREHISTORIC BITES

Fresh Vegetables (see below)
1 slice, whole wheat bread
2 tablespoons whipped Cream Cheese
1 tablespoon yogurt based ranch dressing

Wash the vegetables and prepare them into long thin cut strips. Set them aside.

Cut off the crust of the bread. Flatten the bread by rolling it with a rolling pin on a clean surface or cutting board.

In a small bowl, mix the whipped cream cheese and ranch dressing together. Spread a layer of the cream cheese mixture onto the bread. Add a few of the cut vegetable strips at one end and roll it once. Add a few more strips of vegetables and continue rolling and adding vegetables until you get to the end of the slice.

Pinch the bread a bit to seal it closed. Slice the veggie roll like sushi and serve.

Fresh Vegetables: You can use red, yellow and orange bell peppers, celery and any of your other favorite veggies; cucumber, carrots, baby spinach leaf, baby kale leaf, tomatoes, etc.

Ranch Dressing: The ranch dressing can be swapped for your family's favorite. You can find a yogurt based ranch dressing in the produce aisle cooler at your local Supermarket.

 Did you like this recipe?

RING OF FIRE

1 pound ground turkey
3/4 cup Italian seasoned bread crumbs
1 tablespoon Worcestershire sauce
1 teaspoon dry mustard
1 egg
1/2 teaspoon salt
1/2 teaspoon pepper

1/4 teaspoon onion powder
1/4 teaspoon garlic powder
1/2 cup shredded carrots
1/2 cup shredded zucchini
Ketchup
4 oz. Colby Jack cheese, shredded

Mix the ground turkey, bread crumbs, dry mustard, Worcestershire sauce, egg, salt, pepper, carrots and zucchini together thoroughly. Separate the meat mixture into five equal parts.

Shape each part into a strato shaped volcano and place side by side in a 13" x 9" pan to form a ring of volcanoes.

Use your thumb to leave an indent in the top of each volcano at least two inches deep. Fill each indent with ketchup; drizzle the ketchup down the sides slightly. Bake the "Ring of Fire" for approximately 40 to 45 minutes. Sprinkle the tops of the "volcanoes" with cheese, again drizzling some down and let the "Ring of Fire" bake for an additional 5 to 10 minutes. Let your family see the "Ring of Fire" before serving individual volcanoes for dinner.

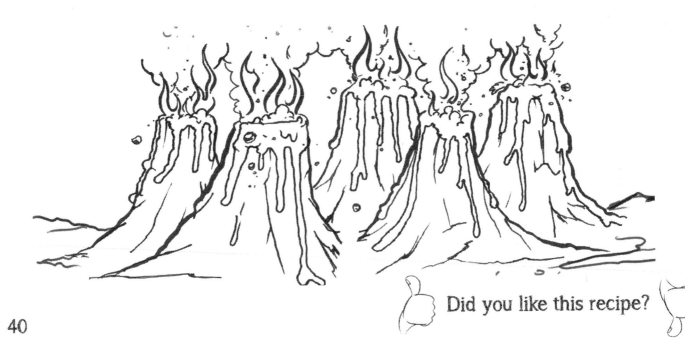

Did you like this recipe?

SLITHERING SNAKE SALAD

12 oz. spaghetti
1 red bell pepper
1 orange bell pepper
1 yellow bell pepper
1 pint grape tomatoes
1 cucumber
8 oz sharp cheese
1/2 cup balsalmic dressing

Cook the spaghetti as directed on the package and set aside to cool completely.

Wash each of the bell peppers. Remove the tops & bottoms & hollow out the center to remove the seeds. cut the peppers into strips & then cut each strip to dice the peppers.

Wash the grape tomoatoes and cut in half.

Wash the cucumber. Slice the cucumber. Cut each slice into quarters.

Cut the cheese into small cubes.

Add the diced peppers, cut tomatoes, cucumber pieces and cubed cheese to the pasta. Toss the entire salad with balsalmic dressing and serve.

Did you like this recipe?

TACO PIZZA

My Magic Meat Recipe (see right)
2 pizza doughs
16 oz. Colby Jack cheese
1/2 cup sour cream, low-fat
1/2 teaspoon garlic powder

Pre-heat the oven to 400 degrees.

Stir the sour cream and garlic powder together and set aside. Finely shred the cheese and set it aside. Slightly oil and flour two pizza stones. Roll the chilled pizza dough directly on to each pizza stone. Equally divide the sour cream and spread it on top of the pizza dough with a spoon to create the first layer leaving approximately an inch around the perimeter for crust.

Evenly distribute the Magic Meat Recipe on each pizza for layer number two. Top each pizza with 8 oz. of cheese to create the final layer. Bake the pizza for approximately 25 minutes, until the crust is golden brown and the cheese is fully melted.

Additional Options: Add a layer of romaine lettuce and/or grape tomatoes chopped before adding the cheese or after it's done cooking and serve.

My Magic Meat Recipe

1 pound ground turkey
1/4 cup onions, finely chopped
15 1/2 oz. can of diced tomatoes or 1 pint of grape tomatoes
1 1/2 teaspoons cumin
1 teaspoon onion powder
1 clove of garlic
3/4 teaspoon salt
3/4 teaspoon chili powder
1/2 teaspoon white pepper
1/4 teaspoon garlic powder
1 cup chopped spinach, fresh

Cook the ground turkey in a frying pan, draining off any excess juices. Add the chopped onions to the cooked meat & 1 clove of fresh garlic (crushed) and continue to cook, stirring occasionally, until the onions are soft. Place the tomatoes into a mini chopper or food processor. Chop until very fine and juicy. Add the tomatoes, cumin, onion powder, salt, chili powder, white pepper and garlic powder to the meat mixture. Chop the fresh spinach in the chopper as well. Stir the spinach into the meat mixture and remove it from the heat.

Quick Tip: Make the meat ahead of time and warm slightly before putting the pizza together.

Did you like this recipe?

TIGER BITES

3 Large Sweet potatoes
1/3 cup light olive oil
1 teaspoon cinnamon
Sea Salt

Heat the oven to 400 degrees.

Rinse, Peel and thinly slice the potatoes. Using clean hands, mix everything together.

Spread a tablespoon of olive oil onto a non-stick baking sheet. Evenly place the sweet potatoes flat along the sheet. Add a light additional layer of sea salt and cinnamon to the top. It's amazing how cinnamon, not sweet itself, can bring out the natural sweetness in the sweet potato.

Bake for 25-30 minutes until the edges of the potatoes are crispy.

 Did you like this recipe?

VEGGIE ROCKETS

4 Sunset Mini Peppers
2 cups chopped romaine lettuce
1/2 cup baby carrots
1/8 cup sunflower seeds
1/8 cup raisins
1 small cucumber
2 – 4 tablespoons of Marie's yogurt based
ranch dressing
1 large bell pepper
1-2 tablespoons cream cheese

Cut the top off of one red pepper
and hollow out the middle.

Slice the cucumber. Chop the
romaine lettuce, ½ cup cucumber,
carrots, sunflower seeds, raisins and
any other favorite salad supplies in
a mini chopper.

Stir the salad dressing into the
chopped salad. Stuff each of the
hollowed peppers with the chopped
salad.

Use a small star shape fondant cutter to create three
veggie stars per rocket out of a different colored
pepper. Simply wash the pepper, cut it into large
strips and use the fondant cutter to create the star
shapes. Glue the stars in place with cream cheese as
the edible glue.

This is a fun salad serve you can pick up and crunch
into.

 Did you like this recipe?

There are a few food experimentation rules that I like to share when I'm visiting kid communities. In fact, if you have visited me to make a recipe, then you just might have heard some of them....

Rule #1: Some recipes are thumbs up & some are thumbs down, but you don't know until you actually try them! This book is designed to get you trying new recipes & food combinations. As you do, you get to vote at the bottom of each page so that you can create your own collection of recipes that you can continue to make.

Rule #2: A recipe can be a VERY POWERFUL TOOL! It can help us get healthy foods into our bodies that we sometimes won't eat alone & when I am visiting kid communities I am always sharing examples from my own counters. So, if you see one ingredient on a list that you don't like, try it in a recipe anyway; you just might find a way to eat foods you won't eat alone.

Rule #3: Your taste buds are always changing as you grow & it's important to keep trying healthy foods that you might not like right now. We had a '10-day try again rule' with my youngest picky eater & she often did discover the change in her taste buds over time.

Rule #4: Cooking is a very important life skill! Even if you only learn the basics, studies have shown that the more kids are involved in the process of cooking & experimenting with recipes, the more likely they are to try new foods & eat healthier.

Rule #5: What if you don't want to try it? Try taking the 'teeny, tiny tinker bell taste!' Yup, that's right....all you need to do is give it a tiny bite to see if you like it or not.

I hope you have fun at the counters experimenting with these recipes, having fun with food discovery & coloring all of the fantastic pages my friend has created.

Don't forget to send me a note about the recipes you like & photos of your kitchen adventures to Jodie@jodiefitz.com ~ I just might share them online!

Have fun in your kitchen mixing it up, messing it up & taste testing new recipes!

Jodie Fitz

P.S. Email me or visit my website www.jodiefitz.com to learn about community visits & to sign up for my newsletter.

Follow along with continuous recipe adventures by connecting with me at...

www.facebook.com/jodiefitzcooks
www.instagram.com/jodiefitz
www.twitter.com/jodiefitz
www.pinterest .com/jodiefitzcooks
www.google+.com/jodiefitz

Made in the USA
San Bernardino, CA
26 March 2018